T0065316

Peace Mongers At War

Bill F. Ndi

Langaa Research & Publishing CIG
Mankon, Bamenda

Publisher

Langaa RPCIG
Langaa Research & Publishing Common Initiative Group
P.O. Box 902 Mankon
Bamenda
North West Region
Cameroon
Langaagrp@gmail.com
www.langaa-rpcig.net

Distributed in and outside N. America by African Books Collective
orders@africanbookscollective.com
www.africanbookscollective.com

ISBN-10: 9956-763-82-9

ISBN-13: 978-9956-763-82-5

© Bill F. Ndi 2018

Table of Contents

War Dogs

The dogs' bark never is fun
Who is now dead and gone
With just the mound left behind
Dazzling everybody blind
To any other story that there is
In their lone struggle to settle in peace

Around a pack of rabid dogs
After them as if hunting hogs
Willing to take blamelessness to the cross
On which innocence is all gain not loss…
For all to wipe their tears
And bury all their fears

In the name of the lamb
Whose light outshines dogs' lamp
Through flesh and blood spilled unjustly
With just hope dogs fall miserably
As the lamb like the tiger strike
And merry make happiness spike.

Seeing with Eyes Closed

Blind I am, the world sees me with my eyes closed
I see the world sees me with eyes wide opened
Not laying eyes on Kah with eyes wide opened
For years, today I did with eyes firmly closed;
This message from the world beyond
Comes to revive the righteous bond.

Blowing Minds

Needed is no extra letter
To take from roses to sores
When roses' fine smell is bitter
Than pricks in thorns' store
To wax human heart red hot
With thoughts one gave it a shot
And shoot we must shoot to smell
And take pricks that trouble spell
Again by positioning better
Letters that otherwise make bitter.

On The Stage

Seeing with the naivety of a child
Laughing raucously like an imbecile
Expressing with the wisdom of a sage
And like a scavenger digging knowledge
Living in this world with the sight of a blind
Who, to see, only does with one thing, the mind
Yelling out like a child parents can't stop
Yelling till he sees the king quake and drop
Finding in you
These Kings will spew…
No, puke! Puke out their guts
Seeing you poets with guts!

Poets' Last Words

They may lie dying
With no words drumming
But their blink
Drives to think
Of their endurance
Seeing no one dance
At the time they hope to see
Their love plunge in liberty…
Off they nod without a word
And our loud cries, their last word!

Outside The Purse

When society loses focus
Her poets and scribes must keep focus
As when in marriage
Woman goes in rage
A dutiful husband must she borne
And if let loose, stolen is the fun…!

Focus for cameraman
Focus for the penman
Focus for husbandman
Focus for businessman
Focus for hunter man
Focus for painter man

Etc…
Etc…!

Focus, Focus, Focus for all man
Focus, Focus, Focus for woman
Keeps world away from loss
And directs the main cause
Our fight would rid of pus
With focus far from purse.

Judge Himself

His robe painted with black blood
His wig whitened with black blood
His crown polished with black blood
His table shined with black blood

His hammer hits black
And black must fight back
For he on black blood cushion rests his back
But self-examining, he won't look back

Hitting the table he shouts out guilty
Forgetting his regalia dyed guilty
On our island of poverty
Making of us poor the guilty

When his forebears were convicts
Just as the poor street addicts
Peddling little antics
Gluing them to street kicks

Tell Mr Judge, "poverty is no crime"
Not even when the poor are his grime
He at least can still intone a chime
That to his peers won't taste like lime

As Lincoln was shocked to see an honest
Man of the trade in his eternal rest
And Mr. Judge needs not do his best
To match the shocking one at rest.

Skin and Heart

Black skin white heart
White skin black heart
All we can change is the skin
Not a heart twisted within.

Shame Game!

Only Van Gogh will handle yellow his way
And none will ever his yellow steal away!
Vagrants brought in something they called development
        Leaving and leaving us in total bewilderment
In mid-air hanging
Left today dangling
Between East and West
Knowing just no rest
In their development finely adorned
Hiding within the rotten king they've sworn
To make glitter their yellow
The like of Van Gogh's mellow
And soothing one transporting to haven
As vagrants' snatching it like a raven
Whose beak stuck in its prey paints
 Our earth red with blood of saints
Saints of innocence and weakness
Who pay the price for shamelessness;
Develop strength to crush without shame
For these blameless are a guilty game
In the Lord's park
Shy of a lark
To caress his ears
As their cry them sears
So must they their necks to find peace
Noose or at gun shot fall apiece
To stop East West dangling
There and then lasting peace knowing.

A shame game!

A shame game
They've always played;
Progress delayed
Where in their own revolution they glory
Of the weak and innocent they make misery
And pray they remain forever blind
In a world the weak prayed all were kind
Even the man eating kings with big appetite
Who in recent years took pleasure in Apartheid,
A monster vagrants supported
Condemning all who reported
This shameful gimmick
These gamers mimic!

Poets to Cook in Butter

Would Eliot did venture
Somewhere near this creature
Some chose for a better half
He'd have picked a saucy calf
To have scared away his dream
For poets to while time up stream;
Idle time for poets he did advocate,
Time our boiling butter won't replicate!
Poets should in this butter rather cook
To give full pleasure to them that look
In hope Eliot's dreams were clowns'
Not these ones lighting up frowns
Through poets' recollections killing time
Which in our lexicon with crime rhyme.

War Pleasure, Child's Revulsion

When a child spends time scanning the horizon
So does a war monger making his a war zone
With their differences in their hopes
The child sets his hopes atop slopes
Where mongers would drag all down
And have them in the stream drown
As the Sun takes its rise
Some pleasure in their vice
Yet, the child sees not the pleasure
'Coz quest for calm is his nature;
With twilights at dawn or dusk
This child will scent in them musk
Awakening him to his dream adoration
So he can stand and show us his revulsion
For our world to see and follow his wisdom
Taking creeds close to heavenly kingdom
Which must on this earth be lived
Not their hereafter believed
For which the blood thirsty do die
Clueless their cause had been a lie…

The Longing

I went round looking and looking for little miss pretty
The one I saw close to home went for pa money
So, never was any deal done
For her desire would be foregone
For I had no money but affection
Which in turn stood miles from her attention
And all I could was pray money bought her some
       Now that I know pretty is not about form!

Welcome miss hideousness if she has a heart
Not like the gun above pointing at a heart
And with desired money can buy a gun
And same money will never drum the fun:
Affection far from her reflection would
Gently soothe any lost soul in the wood
A dream most will like to have
Than live and die with no laugh.

Money Slave

Pursue passion! Slave not for money!
Money that would in you spark cruelty
With illusions of strength and might
Unable to change what a mite
From the poor old widow
Did; having the great bow
For such a wealthy heart
Gladly warming like hearths
With worldly paucity
She possessed cheerfully

Sinuous Curves

Snaking way in with a book called good
The book they drop and carry the loot
And in that book we seek the goodness
In our total state of shabbiness
And God will bless Africa
As he's done for Arm licker
Blessing the dollar mightily strong
Weakening us weak for we've done wrong
Showing the plainness of our nakedness
Plain and naked still filled with happiness
Their Godly right on the dollar printed
Which rights poets on earth would not have minted
Poor poets like poor Africa are poor
And their wisdom like that ancient dour
Chides of the folly of human madness
Strike the chord driving insane mundaneness
To purging mankind of constipated book content
Striking and purging work no poet would ever relent
Until they see these international thieves repent
To repent they must humble themselves
And turn upward the forced downward curves.

Dues for Dews

Morning dew like suicidal on leaves hanging
Frightens not but entices to thirst quenching
After a long night of dehydration
Spent in bed that rocks with commotion
Rocking like the sea hidden within dry fish
That would the sea wave have adorned as a dish
But for politicians happy we're hanged like dews
And for which they would we did pay them weighty dues
And the dues we pay hefty and heavy
With no dew drop touching the ground
Near where our footsteps could be found
Yet, morning dew like liberty would always guide;
Guiding us like a groom his way towards a bride
And unlike a groom with fears of what belies in front
Not fear but joys we shall harbour as a unique front
While dressing a brand new bed with liberty
We shall scan liberty and freely too
With evil oppressors have nil to do.

Tulip Tree Leaves

A tree leaf that says it all
No Bangolanian would fall
Seeing this leaf nor would he stand
And refuse to understand
The call to report back home to ancestors
Who in their graves still grace his life with no gores!
Tulip tree leaf from you I will take no leave
Were the world to care less you were my relief
For those who in you believe the seeds of peace
In them carry the tulip tree leaf of peace
And I bid you! Flourish and flourish!
Even the heart of the Moorish
Desert who rejects the green of your peace
And though its livers do dine on peas

The Fall of Bakassi

When Bakassi fell, France claiming Cameroon
Nothing did say that would his business maroon.
A lesson our morons refuse to learn from
And would ties project to heights top in form
As the French his glass of wine savour
Poor cam marooned ions bleed in labour
Relations between states: interdependence.
Yet, the dependents joy with independence
While their providers dream and dream by a river
From which they cannot a bream take, never ever!
Cameroon, Cameroon, forty-eight years running
Cameroon, Cameroon, forty-eight years crawling;
Sit up and stagger
For you're no toddler
Not just this pen would want to see you
But those you've made poor need to know too
So, this pen may go to sleep
Letting their hearts like frogs leap
And land anywhere in the land safe
And worrying not to be enslaved
As they've known all these years
They have spent shedding tears
You refused to wipe not being brave
For all you are is France's knave!

Encounters

Up for the show,
Everywhere I go,
I do tell them from Cameroon I hail!
And with "a great soccer team" I am hailed
And I would soccer returned stolen flag
Of corruption politicians won't take back
Making every victory in this game theirs
Instead of wiping off the poor their tears
Winning in every game but looking after the poor
And when this game they shall win, poets' pens will praises
pour
And their thirst for them will forever be quenched
As will the poor their imposed pains have entrenched.

Peace Warring War

All   In the metaphysical properties of the Word we believe!

In motion, He sets winds of change in this world: a relief!

Poet:	What do we want?
Audience:	We want Peace!
Poet:	What do we want?
Audience:	We want Peace!
	We want Peace!
Poet:	Where do we differ?
Audience:	They want war!
	We want Peace!
	Peace, Peace, Peace,
	We shall drum Peace!
Poet:	Peace we shall drum
	Drum, drum and drum
	Peace
Audience:	Peeeeeeeeace…!
Poet:	Peace we shall drum
	Until for all mankind
	No pains!
	Peace Reigns!
	Creed is for the cretin
	And what's our duty?
Audience:	Conscience is our duty!
	And Peace shall Reign
	Come sun come rain,
	And Peace, Peace, Peace
	Shall their war shatter apiece!
Poet:	So, What do we want?

Audience:	We want Peace!
Poet:	So, What do we want?
Audience:	We want Peace!
	We want Peace!
Poet:	So, Where do we differ?
Audience:	They want war!
	We want Peace!
	Peace, Peace, Peace,
	We shall drum Peace!
Poet:	And Peace shall Reign
	Come sun come rain,
	And Peace, Peace, Peace
	Shall their war shatter apiece!

True Mother

In the morning a cock crows
A true mother hearing knows
As would cry from her child
When from the heart a child
Does cry
Such cry
A heart pained by Delilah's daughter
Solace does come quick eased by mother
With her words the tears sponging,
Healing broken heart's longing.

Now the heart does know
Who'd the towel throw?

Eve's daughters are not all Delilahs
Not even when their acts echo hers…!

Really Odd

Murderer, murderer kill your corruption!
And from us receive an ovation.
Sad sights on our streets with slain liberty
Your garb colours full bright ignominy
When on innocence your wickedness you unleash
And would the world enjoy it their favourite dish

Murderer, murderer why not kill all wars
To have thanks from us all fill your purse?
With this plague everywhere in our world
Our hopes for lasting peace on fears board
'Coz you can't withstand your thirst for blood
One we come to grade as really odd!

Murderer, murderer your acts kill true needs
For even madmen chastise your deeds
Insane enough for them to reason
And take a distance from their season
Of madness to have us dance with them
          The tune of life plagued with a problem.

Seeds of Peace

You are so tiny
In their world ready
To crush and bury you
With their greed blind to you

Seeds of peace so tiny
The ones I love dearly
To nurture in me the biggest tree
Giving pleasure to the world being free

Under your shade they will sit and stories hear
Of strives and wars nobody will ever fear
For their graves afoot this tree won't your weight bear
And glad we would be with you in us so near

Me, in my grave I'll stroke the root
On which you stand as on good foot
With my remains feeding your leaves
With joy seeing you spread my belief

From birth I bore when all others hope lost
'Coz thin you were and would have entailed cost
Which only patience and faith could come by
Not by their thinking money would you buy

Seed of peace
Tree of peace
Play with the wind the music
That soothes the soul like magic

Fascinating kids and adults
As you had been my catapult
Catapulting the courage and strength
Which in my grave have met me at length

Seeing my dream storybook child love
Flying cherubically above
The buried brutality
They once sang for liberty.

True liberty knows and loves Peace
Not brutalities that them please!
And knowing you all these years, a great bliss
For no good reason I would any dare miss.

Our Big Heads

Big heads multiply their blunder
Canonizing striking plunder
Sapping from the taproot of nations
To leaving nations desperations
Cutting a quarter moon smile on their faces
Forgetting this is just one of the phases
The moon comes up with to blind the night
And spin their heads to see the wrong light
And discard the masses as scums of the earth
Deserving of nothing terrestrial but dearth
Which children in dream tear to pieces
Like the tiger its prey as it pleases
Just the like of heads delighting in the game
Blundering in our streets, looting with no shame
Defining that trade
In favour of eight
Unfolding their blood stained carpet of negligence
On which they display claims of divine providence

Peace Warriors

Vampires shall fly in for a kill
And shall their due have not our will
That has spurn and spurs our undertaking
The one that leaves them shaking and quaking

Vampires welcome for the kill
We shall send you back home ill
When our will has petered your undertaking
Leaving us like tree leaves in sweet breeze, dancing

The Entrails of Thoughts

Philosophy never was wrong
Where human thinking was proved wrong
To thinking thinking needs be in black and white
Whereas black thoughts transferred to us with no blight

Came without ink and sheet
Meeting us in the fleet
With theirs on paper with a pen inscribed
Not ours with the tongue on our minds inscribed

Not with the serpent's hiss
Nor the snaking of the brook its way brooking
Down the valley having us without booking
We would never have missed

Stressing the quintessence of peace
Softening minds like the Golden Fleece
Sweeping away illegitimacy of rule
Our nations were once forced to embrace as a rule.

Strange

Smooth like beauty herself
The cutting edge herself
Sharp like shark teeth
Won't let love breathe
Breathing to grow
Make rivers flow
To their source
Our dream cause
We follow seeing the shimmer
Of such beauty without flicker
Glimmer and dazzle us
To gathering no moss
Strange! Strange! Strange!
Beauty strange
Things does
Makes worse
Hopes by rulers made bad
Hiding figs from the bats
Ignoring leveller will all level
Six feet underground dug with a shovel.

Love Sake

Hit your chest and look at me as a fool
'Coz on me everyone sits as on a stool
Yet, I thought I'd be your throne
Not knowing you'd have me thrown
But as a fallen man I fear no fall
And laugh at sacks of flesh and bones up tall
In pride and arrogance
Only to fall in trance
Moved by the spirit that humbles
So that no soul ever crumbles;
The spirit in the fallen man
Would never leave any man wan!
Instead of hitting your chest
Priding in what's in your chest,
Hug and embrace a poor fool
Whose spirit makes a good stool
On which wise men will sit
For your kind to smell shit
And leave them in a bind
Simply for they're love blind,
Blind for that's the nature of love
And the love buck's always told off.

Our Leaders & Our drums

They came with veils on their faces
We greeted and drummed their praises!
When the wind brought the stench of their faeces
Our nation stood up to halt the disease;
With her our hammers drummed out! Out! Out!
Yet, to cling, cling, cling they crushed the crowd
With their swords chiming a tune
To bash our hopes out of tune;
Hopes whose strength in non-visibility lies
Will the drum beat them out! Out! Out! With the lies
They had veiled with promises to bring in
And unleash their hounds to bite within
Which they do but our hopes are the last words
To usher them out and bury their swords.

His Victory

Seeing shark teeth in display drives to thinking
Of smiles brightening His Excellent thief's win
After promises so untrue and surreal;
Smiling for being propelled to the helm to steal
From the miserable poor, poor miserable misery
Is all the poor plebes are left with as their history
The malapert having his way tricked to the helm
Legates a frightful Jeremiad as an emblem
With brand new egg shells nodding not the doup
Just before they come to see they've been duped.
Behind shark teeth in display is a murder machine
Giving not Rodin's thinker time to support his chin
In pensive moodiness bringing the world to come see
How a sculptor's views dash to and fro across the sea
And His Excellency in this battle won
So, we would acclaim him murderer number one!
When the West his deeds greets those of a strongman
On them we trample as those of a hangman
And sing hangman, hangman!
Your pay is: hang not man!

Farcical Comedy

We hope and wait for too long!
Once the hope and wait come to pass
Then we do suffer too long
Watching politicians stage the farce!

A comedy in agony we borne
Far from the expectations of our entrance
When we came into this world as newborns
With our parents dreaming like lions we shall pounce;

Pounce to shred their foes; lighten their weight,
Burdens brought to bear for they cast a vote
Which per chance made the wolves hates of state
In a world they do treat us as goats

Neither parents nor we are these
And won't ingest their farcical comedy
Funny to those gloom bloom does please
With blowing them out, our only remedy.

Pseudo-pseudo Ephor

We must be dead drunk to always doff our hat
To such a rogue whose every move is so bad!
Moil! Moil! Well known sing song in Cameroon
Where the people's sweat, the ephor's saloon
Keeps cool to his comfort and joys
Of piecing the nation as toys
And how else could he play this game
Being twice shadow of his lame name
Pseudo-pseudo ephor
Makes and makes no effort
To lift his little finger and support
The discomfort; that will steal his comfort,
His birth right not trite
To see all their rite
Perform and have the nation's heart beat
For every threat to become his treat;
Applauded by those behind the mask of his mask
He reigns absolutely and would none anything ask
Now, my people, why sing a song so sad?
Are we deaf to hear it displease the heart?

Anthem for Essigang

O, macaroon covered with poor chicks' feathers
Go sit down and pride yourself in thievery
Like the slums your disgraceful flag shall fly
With your havoc to your name ever true
My father's house that once all tongue could tell
Has now become a house of thieves
So the rest of the world can see
The emblem of the tears of our people

Clan of mbokos, clan of bandits
With death and sadness in our store
Thine be disgrace, thine be great shame
And repudiation for evermore

His Stomach, Our Save...

Each night by the Sanaga crazy Pol drinks
Himself dead not to hear what our country thinks
While we drum the misery drowning us therein
From his sleep we shall have drummed his ear drum thin
For our drums wait not for a natural disaster
To come from this sleazy dickhead minister
Whose brains are in the stomach planted;
A criminal by our drums wanted
For making his stomach our save
Swearing to take it to his grave
Enriching his stomach more than the nation
Keeping the line to honour his devotion
His dream we shall drown before he goes down
And we won't soil our hands to bury his crown.

Dancing with the Devil

All motion and the wind stop
Air's hoarded in a big shop
At the sign of his cut all gasp
Short of air, gasping for a grasp
In hope joy he does bring them
Forgetting him the shame emblem
With whom the dance continue
As man readies to manure
The plants and flowers on his grave
To mourn the departed slave
Money did shuffle and set a dancing
In a handsome world with beauty to sing

Assuring Spell

How could one ever forget this dawn?
The leaves and the grass shout out their joy sun
Running helter skelter from East to West
While the rest of us are being put to test
When in some parts at midnight sun won't set
We all dream to share the joys of their pets
This dawn every year making this motion:
Jubilation over tribulation
Elevating the moods of men
Assuring spells befall governments,
A quiver with new moves of leaves
To empty the devil's sleeves
Stopping the choking dance
Stewing puke as we glance
Calling for a break from division
To sit us up in remission.

3rd Millennium Christmas

Just before Christmas our towns would swarm with life
At Christmas feeding and drinking define life
On Boxing Day, in coffins are our towns
And born again in the malls where funds drown
To revive crunch
That will stall lunch
Undigested wholesome
Near where greed do blossom
While elsewhere eking crumbs
Order of the day slumps.

This Christmas I flew my Fairlane
Passing by their memory lane
Driving me back to the slums
Where never had been seen plums
Yet, their streets only with life stream
This day with just hope of a beam
From the sun that for all does shine
As being in sync with him is fine.

Love Hope

There were ten endless years of wait
Which in them did hide hope as bait
Picked and swallowed were blown in a second
Gone is the mansion of such a fecund
Hope
                              Dope
That once turned our desert green
Now turning our green bloom grim
With eternity to say who was right
Not remembering the endless years of fight
With despair it will never come to pass
Which did and our lesson learned out of class
In which the school of life reserves no formula
To grace the lives of those who swear by the kola
Throwing its peelings to tell our future
Or cast a look at our woe like vultures
Tending to a wounded game on the highway
As hope on us preyed in our wait; such they pray!

Naming the Culprit

Aids, cholera, malaria…
Plague such countries south of Iberia
With responsibility on bad government
The culprit has always had on as garment
Governments that sit not in laboratories
But to poets' nose stinks like lavatories
As they hear of monstrous profit margin
Announced by banks greeted with sips of gin
By CEOs blooming like water lilies in a marsh
Same as the vulnerable poor litter roadsides like trash
Blown together by promises of an end to their plight
In which mix-up they have been told and told they had right
Now to name the culprit, unwillingness or bad government?
Either way the poor lot have to make do with bad government
Unwillingness to let go some change make the rich stable
With the poor longing for their horses they had a stable
Longing for the culprit? Name names it is a muddle
Stephen Blackpool would never have sought for a model!

Our Success

Countries end up!
Mine in a cup!
For the best we do is abdominal
Lifting of the cup in way practical
To a fowl after quenching her thirst
Mechanical sports in which we're first

French tip, *pot de vin*
Cameroon tip, vain
Potamology finding one with water
But that big river overflowing with beer
Play the game, shake your skin
And you are a great kin

In this land where water must taste bitter
The bitterer the water the better
In benumbing the bitterness by foreman
Devoid of regard, brought to bear on man
Go round the world such numbness
You'd never find with success!

This Duet

Fellow would-be dead poet
Treason sung as a duet
None would want to sing
But this is your thing

For even if you were slain and slain
Your blood will leave indelible stain
On the hands of our blood thirsty guru
Whose evil thinking and cruel deeds do brew

A pot of hemp to deaden the crew's senses
To executing their pointless performances
Having the nation on her knees on a rough surface
And would love us to project this as a smooth surface.

Sing and sing out the hurt
Till guru stops to flirt
And by the horn tackle the bull
And give our nation a kind pull.

Gimmicks King Commander

He only saw himself, chief commander
And how could he get there? Gerrymander
His way to the boxes
Leaving us with losses

He got there!
We are here!
Neither of us blind to that gimmick
Of his rendering the nation sick

Year in year out
He goes not out
Like a canker worm
Eating within form

To leaving the carcass
Of our love no feathers
But wanting us ostrich proud
Thinking us fools in a crowd

But we are a crowd conscious of being fooled
And out of the mess will have ourselves pulled
Even with all his riggings and gun-totting
Hoping we'll yield and yield; that's not our thinking!

Fighting Boredom

In his mad rage bin laden
Stirred the world and two Dutchmen
Reminded me my Old English lesson
In Belgian Bruges spelling out the reason
For facts so horrendous for being loaded
Truckies in Fleming always drive loaded
Projecting the rage on their roads
With trucks jumping about like toads
Discovering the sun or uniformed junkies
In a shooting rampage to protect poll flunkies.

Jocular Dutchmen all jocund
Didn't seem to think I will reckon
Their joke as a recluse isolating himself
Loaded with tons and tons of many little elves
Buzzing like bees in the head of the insane
Driving bin laden to plod his way through the mountain
Docking himself under the rocks after such a crime
Leaving our world under the spell of madness begrimed
To cleanse the dirty ousting of bloody gore
And save America from leadership bore

Mobilization and pressganging the press
Must defamation align to all impress
Both U and your N did fall in the trap
To have been avoided by one Von Trapp
Carried away by the sound of music
That its grip on the world held like magic.
Yet, Ben and Adolph's blasts the world frighten
For they won't want any sound to the mood brighten

Same as to sweep boredom bush commander in chief
Goes to sweep the streets of Bagdad to leave grief.

No Trip from their Strip

Happy we killed the devil
Is nonetheless killing still.
We were of God chosen!
Clouds shade this reason.
My pen shed tears
With mourners fears
The next drop takes not him
As every hope grows slim.

Peace of mind dwells far from their strip
With no chance given for a trip;
Return or of no return
Stay under fire and burn
Translating our wickedness
Light years from human kindness
Their kill they bury out of our screen
Like red blood cells waste in the spleen.

Look further south for diversion
With those clowns set for distraction
Their fart stinks more than our shit
So we must their fart's throat slit
To secure the scented perfume of our waste
For which no rooms open for a truce but haste
To dazzle the world with swords' glitter in the sun
So not the reflection of the Heart of my Sun.

Those days when life was up and kicking
I didn't think I would send you to Quiberon
One day I thought I would love find with a run
And it did turn out to be killing
Killing those six years of bliss
Years together I now miss
Ensnared by the flashes of a call
Calls to the heart of darkness appal
And I would you're supreme deity up above
To accept this one time fallen angel with Love
I would rush to the church yard and lay to rest
The regrets I borne now knowing you're the best
And wishing with life I toiled not playfully;
Any offer from you welcomed heartily.

You did see the thorns and my attention call to them
Like young and foolish Yeats found that a problem
And away peacefully walk knowing not
Next day I would live to your name call out
With you lovingly answering
And for explanations waiting
From a guilt stricken heart with remorse covered
Just dreaming the lost best bet were recovered
With remorse in bloom and willingness to sit upright
After such a great fall I stretch my hand without fright
And you and only you alone know what in the cellar
You have in store for this self-confessed appalling fella
In whose dream your righteousness flinches not an inch
As he now makes strides towards you not thinking lynch.

Sowing Gloom

In Cameroon
I hear they drum
They drum in pump
Victory so soon

Receding into the depths
The depths of gloomy black debts
Killing the sound steadily
Their drum breaks increasingly

Our eardrum with such barren seeds
Their victory sows everywhere indeed
And our eyes feast on the noose
They have on us as they buzz

Themselves mad with victory over our wellbeing
Fading their sound till one cannot hear a thing
Like someone once condemned in Russia defied his
country
I'd say not even hanging is well done in this country

Not even with their chants of victory over change
For which in the entrails of our streets we rummage
Till they dig a grave for their victory
Exhuming us to come dance victory.

Armless World

People are dotted with arms
With which they can entreat alms
Some with theirs will push coke for life
The sane only would his pen drive
The world to peace,
Break wars apiece
Cleansing the mind sane
With no one being slain
For pleasure or for fear
His neighbour did arm bear.

These natural arms are by right
For humans to fight their dire plight
Stroke fellow beings with love
Not roasting them on a stove
To derive a ghoulish pleasure
That their world of arms does treasure
To use and force alms out of us
Delighting at seeing their full purse
In their armed nail and tooth world
From which their evil does crawl.

There is more to a world void of arms
Which every human soul soothe like balms
Warming the affected area to heal it
Without them to our daily violence convict
Unleashing peace to run around like hounds
All excited watching their ship aground
In spite armed captains shallow like water
In which we shall neither trade nor barter;

World peace quest is non-negotiable
Were we to be made vegetable!

Inch by Inch.

It was not just the feeling
Inch by inch they came crooking
On their knees

It was not just the sight
Inch by inch they promised no fight
And we went to sleep

Then they started eroding inch by inch
Before we knew they'd signed up for a binge
We'd bidden trouble

So, we signed in for sand bags
They saw in us only rags
They'd shred apiece

In their hopeless design
They dreamt we would resign
We drove them mad

Inch by inch that long awaited feeling
Started creeping in and stimulating
Joys of freedom

Inch by inch their desire
We didn't give them back fire
Leaving them no ash

The storm had come and gone
We have had our job done

Raising the flag of peace

Inch by inch out of the labyrinth
We squeezed the plinth on which stood their myth
And on which Pax fly full mast.

Anguish Donors

In those countries on their thrones,
Kings weigh heavily like stones
Ignoring one king gave up his for the woods
Where hunting he did take waiting for owls' hoots

And were we to change their minds with this tale
Let's quickly tell them before it gets stale
And save the thrones breathing rotten fart
And brighten their face with a fresh start…!

The people are sick of these kings
And would gladly ease their crossings
For if uneasy is the head carrying the crown
A nation with these kings wears nothing joy but frown

When the owls' hoots do come with a big sigh
The relief is that he's gone to the most high
Intimating they whose life's labour
Is in a catalogue of horror

Horrendous nightmare himself
Birthed by leaders themselves
Where all hopes built them protectors
Not their desired anguish donors

Like ripcords on the masses they release
Weights that fall abysmally as they please
Seeing the bottomless pit people's abbot
While in the palace they wait for your vote…!

Plebiscite they would you plebiscite them
When for real you need a pillory for them.

Crowded Sky

I looked up in the sky full of stars
With their dazzles clouding our scars
The constellation gave hope of a new beginning
Our world wedded in matrimony celebrating
Each year the cyclical beginning leaving us in the middle
Surrounded by fallen stars muzzling our efforts in the
muddle

Now looking down here on earth
The darkness deep in kings' hearts' depth
Entombs all hopes of new beginning once birthed
And calls for a split of oneness once contracted
As black hair grows grey so grows this strong feeling
End of scarring buries gloom in good tiding.

Needing not many stars that our heads spin
Like monsters with century old unkempt chins
But just one star to outshine the gloom bringing stars
Whose imprints on man are left flashing behind bars
Taken hostage by fellow man like puppet master
Through the media pulling strings as though nothing
matters

But were this one star to supersede the crowded sky
For simple reasons that this one man has a desire
To choke our world by the throat in his dead struggle
To toil with us and our needs with ease in his juggle
Good tidings we'll seek in the calm darkness of the night
Rejecting every light projected by a dark knight.

Call for a Stomp

Stomping has never been my thing
As for some 'tis their everything
Till I was told a torture star has fallen off
So, to stomping I took and never had enough
Of a peaceful mind never to see any cry
In Cameroon where HE with no law did comply
A welcomed call for a stomp peaceful minds greet
And wish all with me stage this fastidious feat
Stomping out both them and their every filth
That transformed our fertile fields in a heath.

Stomping is now my thing
I would everyone's thing
Done with pleasure to shield the victims of torture
In a New World not of their order in future
A world in which the rivers of tears have run dry
With the new easy head upholding the crown high
Glittering the light from the heart that warms like hearth
Not the one of yore that stung hearts like poisoned darts
With craft misappropriated for abuse
Our dream and fight for peace put to disuse.

Mine Fields

In the fields mines sprouted like mushroom
Just like that which none wants to know: gloom!
Placing them there cost peanuts
Watching them devastate hurts
Not just the amputee but the onlooker
In total shock if maker is a hooker
Taking robbers as well as saints
Minding only the scores she gains.

Hooker onlooker budge an inch and save the world
Seeing the dangers of this ill why not spread the word?
Or are you for the end waiting to celebrate?
Deadly acts none would relish to commemorate
As you do and I just want to know if you would your member
Chopped with doer looking as if there's nothing to remember
When in deed he's got all to answer for your fate
Which to you we would project not your game of hate

Such is the game you have played and played us all
And now we ask not for more but to see you fall
And if we have not the strength to dislodge you
We will bring to mind time coming to our rescue
At least time your guns cannot fight in their blindness
As that of your mines killing us with cheerfulness
Filling our measure with gloom unbearable
In your vast mine fields that's indescribable.

Let the Poems Bee

Let these few lines be
Let them sting like bee
Let the poems speak more than I do
Let the poems guide more than they do
Let the poems bridge the gap they've created
Let the poems talk for the voiceless instead
Let the poems be the waves washing off our coast in rage
Let the poems be David fronting Goliath in his rage
Let the poems be the songs we shall sing tirelessly
Let the poems be songs' wrath falling mercilessly
Let the poems be the spears to bring down all tyrants
Who sit and dream none will issue them warrants
Let the poems be a funny clown with his smile on kids' face
Such on which tyrants have misery constructed in their craze
Let these poems be the wind that sings so loud
So loud, bringing peace to the slaving cloud
And falling all the trees engrained in tyranny
Against all the poems standing for veracity

Upon the Verdict

On our side
Verdict from posterity
Unspeakable
To the expanse

Magicking forward
To draw attention
To anything grid
They trample on

With joy at seeing
Our world fall
Free of embrace
From a world

Neat and tidy,
Rid of arms clutter
Fall throwing givers
In fastidious feat

They and only they
Pleasure to misery in
As the rest of the world
Slopes into their court.

Treasure we shall
In posterity's verdict
Against our own misery
Not their earthly glory.

Dream

Wonderland where in a second an eternity we live
Horror land where in an eternity a nightmare we live
Coupled with our miserable daily lives with the mares
We would in the endless time of a second one fares
Not this blade edge waking us to the harshness of reality
Not until our world comes to an end dreams give hope
heartily
Especially when it comes to burying a nightmare in one
To waking up in a world void of a tyrant our demand
What other dream would we want having had all along
These scary loads on our head like dragons from Hong
Kong?

A Hopeful's Day

After a dark night of gruesome nightmare
With the head all empty and left threadbare
The unchanged sunlight follows his aged old tradition
So do hopefuls embrace dictates from tyrants' mansions.

Sitting by such a stunted tree
Like a child hoping to be free
With the fall of a fruit to send him wild
After standing the mess tyrants have piled

Year in year out drifting away
All hopes as well being swept away
Under this tree crushed stunted
By tyrants' weight subjected

The ocean in them with dryness bloom
The stream ran to their core leaving gloom
Lighting up the hopeful's day
Drudging without any pay

And tyrants smile their hearts beat
So nations are free to bleed
When gangsters strive in their mansions
Just as outside strives starvation

Under whose shed a people lament
Tyrants' gift to them for enjoyment
And one day lament will give way
Give way to their comfortable stay

What thinking drives the hopeful to this?
None has ever out of thirst drunk piss!
But all at some point dreamt of bliss
On that day they'll have a fun kiss!

Hope hopeful hope
See cupful scope
With the night in arrogance striding
To brighten thought of nightmare looming

Above tomorrow's sky burning and scalding
To eventually fade when comes the evening
From whose bosom rises a smiling constellation
Hopefuls copy innocently for consolation.

The Bee's Business

One day,
One day
This tree will give way
Running around play
Fully free none bemoans
And joyfully none mourns
But glee and glee
A dancing tree
Freshens and soothes within
Like hearts honey pumping
A bee must come protect
Not the spoil sport elect
Who would this dancing tree fell
Only to hear jingle bell
Obstinately chime
The state of our clime
With no fair weather
Skinning our leather
To grace these clowns of power
For they're would-be war wager
Hitting heads up against the wall
Forgetting their acts do appal
The busy bee his business minding
Saying why bee gives tree dancing
Room for all the gloom
Bees would sweep with broom
And have real honey flow
Where they would money flow

String Puller

The French? Yes, the French are good
To get us, they hoard our food
No, our petrol
And pay patrol
To put on our thrones brigands
Well trained in their bands
To play just the music they love to hear
And when we run away from home of fear
To their street well lit
Our eyes without lids
Send shock waves to the hearts
Lighting streets without paths
All amazed at the deeds
Spreading money like seeds
In lights stolen from the pavements
With us dreaming not of payments
As the floor of our pockets welcome
Kiss from misery brought by a cent's calm
When the French had invited us
All we left behind was curse
Now with knowledge they feed our killers
That's why they can't save us from these killers
That's why they are goooooooood: ubiquity
Outright excuse from responsibility
And the French?
That's their stench!

One of 5 That Beat 187

Little by little
They spotted dimples
With some before me plodding the beautiful avenues
Those by the Champs-Elysées with so little revenues
Wondering the burning lights in the streets, blind
Where misery plodded hoping for a kind
Mind to embrace
From other race
Without ruffle
Without shuffle
And no thought
Of law or tort
By a palace
With just one place
For a big gun that shoots
Far beyond to kill shoots
In lands so distant
That none a deviant
Would dream but greet a great five
In a council ninety-five
Gets not close to a vote
Where there's no antidote
For bullies had been born
And others can't be sworn
Within the walls impervious to change
Change's not for the castles but the grange
For farmers to till and toil
Not because they own the soil
But are the soils to be shaken off
For these nations to have air enough

In unity they are democratic
For the sixth one just has to boot lick
And if not, all his kind are with sanction
Greeted for they're champions of corruption
Refusing to hold its light
For five to have burden light
'Coz nature designed them on top of this one
To be split apiece as they build block as one
To blacken black, black
When one goes off track
The track of gloom
Set as their boom
Down the spiral
Artificial
Street walls
Like falls
Falling
'n crushing
This black sheep
Bleating sleep
Out of their desire
To forget the fire
They lit to burn black, black
And hail their life with cracks
Revolution can only be white
When 'tis black it is covered with blight
So five must beat one eight seven
What? Five are right to break even...!

Keeping the Bag Clean

house

ee too

carries a stamp of…
mad house
for gliding
by bunny
down the palace bed stealthily
squandering all our capital
from the streets of the capital
giving king heir
that is unfair
and as such a hair in our soup
for which I wouldn't you stoop
but if you would, like me, puke !
and fear not the might of nuke
then the house can see clearly
we don't eye them blissfully
so they can take their stamp out
for which act we greet no pout
but smiles and smiles for dirt-free
freedom their stamps carved for fee
on a spree to shop sending
bunny who knows just spending
building foundation to drag
our country down like a rag
madness for which we can't brag
and must it keep out of bags!

Sing Them Out

On the brink of survival hovering precipitously
And for the drudgery they take no responsibility
And we long and long hours in the fields drudge to bind
Our national tragedy haunting with no mind

Beasts of burden they have made us all
And would at their sight all of us crawl
And like the lines of poetry we shall so do
For if not our potency they will steal too

For though a verse glides smoothly on line
It neither tells lies nor accepts wine,
Steps not on line like our heads on us
Willing we carry them like a cross;

Wine that maddens they who act unkind
Stripping us of our thin coat of rind
Let our verse do averse them at will
Let our acts like verse our venom spill

Then kindness shall tickle their crowded brains
Preventing our singing in the plains
Songs of peace and freedom they won't hear
To protect the gun merchants' big fear

To stay out of business for a song
Burying their slogan, "guns make you strong"
Which won't hold true for us nor our verse
With such argument our plight's a curse

Yes! Man-made curse is our plight for sure
And our position its only real cure
Where at the brink of freedom we'll sit
After having dealt away with their shit

Thrown precipitously in latrine
Savouring sweetness of verse not quinine
Human hearts we shall lift up sky high
And the fall they sought after will fly.

Ghost Haunting Ghost

In that palace was a ghost who tortured
And tortured us by endorsing a venture
To readjust such structures all blackened
By this ghost by the others being shaken

The ghost of ghost towns haunted king's palace
Which news quickly got to the big palace
In which sat king god of France for fourteen years
And out of fear he dashed out to spread fears

Went soliciting the world and her bank
To leave this ghost on our river bank
Rather than chase the haunted ghost our town's
Would left palace and be drowned down the downs

By the by generations to come will
After this ghost inherit big king's will;
Their burden easing church's first daughter
cleaning no dust though carrying the duster

King god would rather protect his off-spring
By embracing the best art of smearing
Which his game it has been to down many
A voice from the revolutionary

Stubborn to the bone showing he knows all
About why king god had to make a call
For the world to use her bank to free ghost
'Coz with rebel they joy not at us roast.

Master or Monster

Transformation is the devil's act
Transubstantiation a Christian pact
That one did broker with our great nation
And was made master to head the nation

As master, claws he did pop out
Giving the nation to the draught
Like a master throwing his dog a bone
Which draught now hits hard this nation like stone

When we brought him in, we hailed, "Master, Master!"
Now wanting him out, we cry, "Monster, Monster!"
Knowing now what to think
Would you told us one thing:

Beauty, hiding cloak for monsters!
Ugly thoughts to have of masters!
They the devil's acts condone
Hoping to have pact undone!

Ordering high corruption
They would we have communion
Praying for corruption incorruptible
As if there is nothing inevitable!

The Broker

calls both calls all
makes of their fine-looking crime
that which in human is slime
and tells them all

        both could let fall such
        with courage not Dutch
        in between two stools
        ordered not in schools

for want of peace
governed with ease
by organising the fall
of all that they could not let fall

        weapon they carry for fear of fate
        that will end up engendering hate
          to cleansing ethnicity
        with men's blood flooding city

    streets with them behind castle's walls
        caring not this shock wave appals!
broker equity
in simplicity

    and see the colourful tie of peace fly
    up high in the sky as all comply
        leaving not one with the voice of ten
      to brace strange dreams flooding his ken.

Master of Disaster

Action your pillow
Ne'er will ye be low
Rest, your head will find
You'll know peace of mind

By word and action
Deny his auction
Bid to fake buyers:
Multinationals

With claims of fair trade
To leave you in straits
Where earthly master
Like ours disaster

Calls in for greedy
Cull of the needy
Strength you should come by
For all to quest why?

The word in you grow
Strength and courage glow
To out do all foes
Who walk on tiptoes

Through your weaknesses
To crack crevices
In which master falls
The like of man's balls

Wrath Of Time

His sneeze once jitters and chills sent us
World ignorance thought this won't end thus
And today brought home how time has nibbled
His strength making big bully a cripple

Perfect grace in humility
He accepts with stolidity
As for you and I brave not his craze
And by such never will we be dazed

If our tyrant master does what we have done
No wonder our nation would happiness borne
Not before he releases his grip on power
A feat which to him will only his pride lower

With a kiss of the humbling tumbler from which we
drink
He would his obstinate pride avoid with him do sink
As he struggles to cling on to a deadly foe
Our nation will see how to himself he brought woe

Time having wrought what no human hand would
Even with a lifetime spent carving wood
The nakedness of time's equitable ire stands tall
As yesteryears' standing tormentor embrace his fall.

Our Dullness Their Happiness

I have seen all the sights
I have heard all their fights
And have been told sheep are stupid
Made to believe their brains morbid
Until this night an ewe and a ram
I saw on a freeway by a farm
Having themselves sneaked away
Like Romeo and Juliet their way
Made this night fearless of cars
As if to say nothing mars
Love so pure as the wool on their back
Will have no tiger to make them crack
As our car did slow down, they did pause
And moved on as though nothing their cause
Would shake, the meekness they lent to a lord
And for generations have kept on board
Meekness lack of foresight has styled dullness
With which rams, ewes and lambs know happiness
In the wildest dreams of the majority
Far removed letting thrive acerbity
My pen's tears put up a duel to sweeten
At night of in daylight it will happen.

A Country's Fame

                    Their hearts joy to see others mourn
                 As their parents killed and won't mourn
                    And some of ours near the Equator
                       In these shoes desert in a squalor
Those blacks looking like parents' game
Which now earns the people their fame
Lazy
Muzzy
First nations
Feed passions
Shameless hate for these disenfranchised
Whose only rights on earth are their cries.

Words, Thoughts, Flames & Calm

Words piling up after words
They pile up to bury swords
They bring freshness forever
Flowing from our Peace River
From whose banks no money grows
As the cool breeze of calm throws
Away the dirty leaves Fall
Helped to erect war's wall tall…!

Thoughts piling up after thoughts
They pile up to strike the chords
Chords that hype us and rain calm
Which in our hearts bring no qualm
When the rest has all gone wrong
Peaceful thoughts of peace make strong
The mind warring thoughts of war;
Weaken and make an outlaw…!

Flames burning and burning bright
Does shine the way to man's plight
Polluting politicians
Sowing their seeds of deviance
They wish like mushrooms do sprout
And intoxicate the stout
Stout with resolve to keep cool
Though he never went to school…!

Calm settling in after calm
Letting flow a soothing balm
Glossing human face with joy

Burying that their dirty ploy
That ruffles precious desires
They live to drag down the mires
Overflowing with resolve;
One to live with problems solved.

Gold Blind

When gold blinds shit glitters
Where peace reigns blade slithers
Not but by accident
Any who dissident
Might be with his bee sting
To the world upsetting
Upsetting dissident
Won't that shit smell as a trend

Where dissident are blind
Gold getters treat all blind
Guide them down stream to drown
For with sight they'd kick crown
Not for kicks but for real
Giving their world a thrill
Letting nothing to blind
From before nor behind.

Litany of Lamentations

Not just a vicious cycle
I would say a spiral of violence
Not just psychological torture
I would say a nation run by thieves
Not just crushing of youth's dream
I would say killing of the larvae before they grow
Not just a wall made of gangsters
I would say constructed with their bricks of arrogance
Not just haughtily bawdy
I would say morally uncouth
Not just devilishly cunning
I would say satanically sly
Not only the smell of their shit
I would say the stench of rottenness
Not just looking like political mishmash
I would say political indigestion
Not just misery in squalor
I would say abjection in a quagmire
Not just legalisation of corruption
I would say bastardisation of impurities
Not just condoning crime without punishment
I would say consolidation of their heinousness
Not just a throne and crown in decay
I would say their timeless putridity
Not just a king sowing seeds of discord
But I would say but dances and rhymes with division
Not just clannishly sheepish
I would say gangsterly arrogant
Not just sloppily clumsy
I would say a thousand headed hydra

Not just monstrously ugly
I would say a basking shark
Not just the flames of passionate hate
I would say unpardonable hellish hate
Not just that they can't change
I would say they've made up their minds impervious
Not just they won't look back
I would say some men can't just change
Not just trapped in their quick sand
I would say misery, poverty and privation
Not just a gang of petty thieves pushed by hunger
I would say highwaymen robbing for greed
Not just a lazy stupid bunch at the helm
I would say a lousy crazy bunch steering the ship aground
Not just a demagogue thinking he's a pedagogue
I would say a coward with demagogic delirium
Not just fake politicians and statesmen
I would say convoluted to the marrow bone
Not just their disorderly debauchery
I would say chaotic apocalypse now
Not just driving the nation into her grave
I would say making of every life living hell
Not just through blind and questionable greed
I would say through reckless and unthinkable felony
Not just by burning and burning with fire
I would say burning and burning to ash all hopes
When the gangster in chief has to this listen
I would the world ask him what he has learnt as a lesson.

Oddities, Odd, Odd, Odd…!

When it shines, rains
Heats up or cools down
My people are under fire
My people bleed blood

When they're in pains
Heads would see them drown
My people are in the mire
My people drown in the flood

When stars cheer plains
Our heads would all frowned
My people listen to the lyre
My people dare have a thought

When heads have stains
They flag colour brown
My people become great liars
My people are charged with fraud

When the poor strains
He looks to the crown
My people become whingers
My people must be fought

When head disdains
He looks like the clown
My people eye with laughter
My people must this wrought

When shame abstains
We see him drag his gown
My people won't be made friars
My people should face court

Refrains

And man's
         binging
                  Until then,
             little
                  by
                      little
                                  firm
As though by nature all is susceptible
At the helm
Unchanging
Binger
                        Looting
Rooting

                                          Our future
                                          In a spiral
Growing   on   the
bank
                                          Not of a river
                  But that of this world
                  Drowning many a helpless
                        Lad's refrains
                        And leaving them
                        That are binging
                        Within the walls
Of one street
Leading home
Sick home
Adrift;
I must shift.

Far From The Western Front

Dead silence in the fields
We hear of
Knowing not we'd need shields
To fight off
The king of corruption
Who's fair skin
With wanton impulsion
We're just skin
His muzzle sweeps across
The country
Leaving behind just dross
And for free
You can see why we fear
No bully
Who would we took the rear
Being lonely
When in unity strength
Certainly
We'd have to find at length
Willingly
Away from noisy fields
We shall trust
No king from their sword guilds
Whose gold rusts.

Their Heir Not Our Air

Break the broke down with clubs
Guide the poor to the pubs
Leave them no tropical fresh air
Until for him is found an heir

Dancing to the tune of country
Music warming hearts of con tree
Hill Bullies blind to virtues
On the path of war, real truce

Holding the bloke out of every club
Keeping him away from every cup
And salvage the country in a mire drowning
Leaving no possibility of running

Spoil sport won't escape this fate
For others he lay down hate
But the pen above hate flies
Noting the country's cries

Noting our country's cries
Pens do more than heave sighs
They prick the country to the pain
The pain she would everything slain

Once up and aware of ill
Unwanted heir's sent uphill
For freshness to sweep the plain
For all to breathe without strain

DBT The Griot

The griot is one in a kingdom
Beyond sentient wisdom
  I knew myself
Not a naïve self
Only full of trustfulness,
      Trustworthiness,
          And more which this griot to me
           Pointed as the road to tragedy
          Badly needed for inspiration
        Without which all is desperation
              To the hero and his creator
One with other
                Neither an impostor
Like son taking after father
        Tragic heroes
        Let flaw flows
        The like of tears
       Purging our fears
     To see through him our misery
    Which our heads won't have as history…!

                Undated.

A
Cell
Phone

What a marvel
Andrew Marvel
Would love to use
To accuse abuse
Telling his mistress
To chase his distress
For today no one would
Venture into the wood
To hear a poet lament
About dirty garment
Kings need not have
Cutting in halves
Meagre rations
In our nations
Reputed
Polluted
With this new weapon
We rely upon
As one for mass instruction
Not this Miss Education
On human ears welded
Shining like a gilded
Bazooka ready for a kill
Like kings executing their will.

Burning Hate

Hate of state dressed in ostrich feathers
Fooling us he's better than burglars
In his pride unwilling to see any triumph
Anywhere near or around this village trough
His feathers so bright
Must attract a bride
And if not his might will
Without which he's to kill
'Coz his feathers fail to magnet
For he is the only magnate
With god-given right
Heeding not our plight
Good reason all should stand and chant
And if he won't cave in, then rant
To beating the drum he would praises beat
Until he slops down from his lying seat
Shedding off those ostrich feathers
To take this heat brought by his blear weather
That has killed streams and their banks
Or better still with them all funds sank
Being afloat in their dust let none drown
With gifted wisdom Man stands his ground
Not handicapped as most men are
Placing disability far
From the strength and ability
Birthing full possibility
Buried by this hate
Burning all our state!

Feeding the Baobab Tree

Though fresh it looked
Anger it hooked!
From whence it's seed
Given no heed
For being tiny
Chose trendy
saw

across

this ready

remedy

applause !

that baobab tree

sat in our yard

many centuries

yes it grew fat

and we grew thin

and it came to pass

it swallowed in

not our bright stars

our lamentations

fed it this fat

not confrontations

nor aims with darts

yet, it brought us together
to sit, stories tell and hear
know
no
saw!
To slit our throat
For shame's clean coat

By our leaders worn
For which they're not sworn.

Flower Pot Music

Would   no   one   tell   the   world
  Of   melodious   mused word
    Adorning   my   computer
Singing so sweet potted flower
Music   no   one   hears
Even those with ears
But the eyes on which she strikes the chords
Softly and carefully against odds
The pot the drum
Does the heart plumb
The flower
The drummer
Sending one up the ladder of joy
And up he should go without being coy
Ready to feast the eyes
Like a child sighting rice
Without price weighing on his kind
In a world none has him in mind
Safe flower pot drumming colour
Spurring tears of joy not dolour
Saying why no one hears
'Coz the lot harbours fears.

Depredation

The wind did sing change in the North
Dragging the North down to the South
North now down South
South not up North.

For better life hereafter
South must bear the weight
With promise to wait
When Northern wealth breaks rafters…!

Change shall come South
Burying livers in the swamp
Of misery bright without lamp
This with no doubt…!

Crying out loud
Blacks need not have lived centuries ago
Here today, see what was here years ago
The big, big crowd…!

We've won keeping all the same
If they wish they can cry
All we know is, we'll fly
That's what accounts for our fame…!

Lions on their strength depend
Weaker preys can only complain
Which will not take away their pain
Predators can't repent…!

Freshness they did not call for
As pasture and prey flourish
Predators need not nourish
Acts of emotions in their store

One of them once said
You don't kill, you die!
Which was just a lie!
For which he was paid!

When his time was up death came knocking
His strength and wealth could not help
Yelping a scold at the whelp
Who his sunset forced that evening.

Coming of The Vultures

I would start with Poland and Turkey who're sick
Theirs were far from such bushes as ours thick
And aggrandisement gave vultures a kick
When these countries chose to take their dick

The vultures having kept watch over their sick
Got tired and flew in from the West with a trick
Painted white, they carried crosses on each beak
We sensed not they were coming to our graves dig

Wildebeest we were styled
On us the load they piled
For we were just beasts of burden with smile
And all they did us was just to revile…!

Realising we won't succumb to being their spoil
They did work out a way, a way to recoil
Leaving us assassins to make sure we toil
Toil we do toil day and night on our own soil

From this they have taken and do take all
In a mad struggle to see we all fall
Rushing to pay for our blood in the mall
Prices we do find too far, far from call

I'd like to end for Poland and Turkey got well
And before they knew they had no sick man they'd shell
So these vultures made our land receiver of the knell
Yet, their greed told them not this day they'll be in Hell.

Of Strands and Strength

I let my hair grow in strands
They saw it grew with my strength
All they could, they did stand
To see this hair short in length

Short the hair was close to the skin
Atop my head they found a drum
To drum life out till I was thin
Guess what! They ignored it a bomb

Long in wait for this day to come
Which now has come for the action
They would my sound were soft and calm
To their sleazy inaction

But I would they drum my head more
For my joy at the sound pricking
The heart of wickedness's store
Built and protected by our king

Skin of my head not skinhead skin
Wonderful music does stream out
Nothing blows away, not the wind
But she pulls together the crowd

Stormy wind moving clouds in haste
Casting no doubt to the faithful
Who to his strands and strength stays chaste
Tunefully filling our heir full

The length of this hair the wisdom
Like gold mine masked by the dumpster
In our country made a kingdom
Subjects are ruled by a gangster

Peaceful Lake of Peace

This peaceful lake of peace is in Ndop
There, the rice field green better soothes mankind
In which lake, for a swim war can't drop
As Christians, Muslims and animists bind
Their strength in being to each other
Kind and would go a step further
They would go this step to embrace
Embrace each other not their craze
Driving our world to the extremes
We woke up to find were not dreams
Crashing on towers high as Babel
And ringing of madness its warning bell
Greeted by the West with madness
Which does steal away happiness
With just thought of lake burning its flames
So sane should avoid shifting blames.

Their Gift

Never did we call for change;
Not that we didn't need change.
They came with promises to brighten our days
Swayed, we welcomed their darkness; it killed our stay!

In which darkness we grope
While they laugh at our hope
Attempting to fly without wings
For they've impressed on us new kings

These new kings, parvenus, hug swords
Those of darkness that won't kiss words
But glory amidst misery blooming
Like rose in those days in spring morning.

Though our seasons are dry and wet
Our days welcomed bream in our net
To feed our flight high up above
Now by kings burnt on a stove

Whence of yore she by the hearth bask
And together we filled our cask
With godly nectar to gladden hearts
Not these burns driving home bitter hearts

Death Drover

Low live tyrant, you trash up my people
Like a slave you please those in that circle
Where they found you brain dead
Making you to cart death…!

This injection, I pump not into you dead horse
Those around you have a fight for a good cause;
The death you bring them buries not its essence
For, from their graves it shall sprout in abundance…

Yours mightn't think you a slave
'Coz you live not in this cave
But this dirty job of carting death
Falls far below slaves' material dearth.

Slaves work for nothing
So they need nothing
Not even the life of misery that's theirs
But tyrants like you we would all drown in mires.

Crazy Bushfire

Misery I have known all my life
But bushfires left such scars in my life
With no place for plastic surgery nor divine
Interventions to gladden hearts like wine
But the pains of burns endured to the end
Cut short the prayers they started and didn't end
To my grave, I will take these prayers
Inferno did lead their hopes astray
But their prayers I'll continue so they know no end
Till saints burnt in the fire were to be back on earth sent
Or again till from their ashes they did rise
So for others' madness no life will be the price.
How could Yeats be wrong man created death
When man his conscience traded for dearth?

Wind Sings to the Trees

When the wind gently blows trees don't nod
disagreement
Dancing her soft music calls for no disagreement
Unlike our kings whose open mouths do bring storms
Uprooting trees and leaving not even their stumps
With populace all dragged in heavy chains
And led to far off lands afoot mountains
Where to them intone are dirges for joy
Soft and gentle accomplishing a ploy
For kings' happiness at tolling the knell
Which they do joy at hearing masses yell,
Yelling at daunting evil incarnate
Bringing before them such never seen hate
Where kings are meant to be noble at heart
Preserving nations from being torn apart
Like wind's music calling us by our name.
When this shall come to pass, so shall kings' fame.

When we intone our music for kings' dancing
Pleasure, at us, they cruelly start biting
Hoping we'll cower and stoop low to their
Hellish hope to inter our dreams to fare
In a land never before promised man
But such promise we must make sure we can
So kings' storm will never bring to shore waves
Or would do so to sweep them to their graves
Then the gentle breeze that sings to tree leaves
Would sing and hailed with our sighs of relief
For change shall have come
To us full-scale calm.

We Shan't Perch

kill   peace slyly
her music has just
far from dust
been really
soft so
and called for no
knell, bell, snell, cell, gel,
smell, yell, spell, girl, fell…
shot hunting change for all
but stood tall,
treating waste matter
she is a master
no mistress
would with mess
So she won't look
nor utter a yelp at the fluke
blinking bs
on whom should be unlocked swarms of bees
to buzz change with e in their ears
and hoping one of their ears hears
not the soft music
but the pain with which all is sick
of them dreaming in silence we die
round the clock we shall tell them they lie
for we are birds from hunters flying
if power-tricksters think themselves hunters shooting without
missing
we shan't perch
as we for peace search.

Quaker Tapestry

Tapestry of peace
Blowing just cool breeze
Caressing human eyes
With warmth and no cold ice
The wicked may on it stomp
                              And stomp
But its measure fills cups
With joys and no hiccups
For the tranquillity of the mind
So soothing to the sight of the blind;
Quakers forge on
Leave wars forlorn.

Printed in the United States
By Bookmasters